LIGHTNING BOLT BOOKS™

Endangered and Extinct Fish

Jennifer Boothroyd

Lerner Publications Company
Minneapolis

For Jack
-J.B.

Lerner Publications Company
A division of Lerner Publishing Group, Inc.
241 First Avenue North
Minneapolis, MN 55401 U.S.A.

For reading levels and more information, look up this title at www.lernerbooks.com.

Library of Congress Cataloging-in-Publication Data

Boothroyd, Jennifer, 1972–
 Endangered and extinct fish / by Jennifer Boothroyd.
  pages cm. — (Lightning bolt books™ — Animals in danger)
 Includes index.
 ISBN 978-1-4677-1331-3 (lib. bdg. : alk. paper)
 ISBN 978-1-4677-2494-4 (eBook)
 1. Extinct fishes — Juvenile literature. 2. Endangered species — Juvenile literature. I. Title.
QL617.7.B66 2014
597.168 — dc23   2013019750

Manufactured in the United States of America
1 — PC — 12/31/13

Table of Contents

Fish

Fish are special animals. They have backbones. They use gills to breathe underwater. They have fins.

Fish use their fins to swim.

These bluefin tuna are endangered.

There are many types of fish in the world. Some are endangered. Endangered fish are in danger of dying out.

5

Endangered Fish

Winter skates are found in the Atlantic Ocean. They have long tails. These fish can grow up to 5 feet (1.5 meters) long.

These fish are dying out. Too many people have caught them for food.

Winter skates swim in shallow water. **They glide along the ocean bottom.**

The winter skate is nocturnal. That means it is more active at night.

Look at this huge fish!

The Atlantic goliath grouper can grow more than 7 feet (2 m) long.

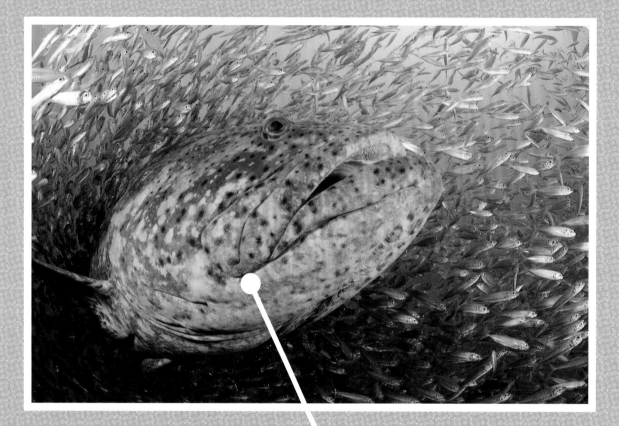

Someone caught an Atlantic goliath grouper that weighed 680 pounds (309 kilograms)!

The Atlantic goliath grouper can have more than three rows of teeth.

Not many of these fish are left in the wild.

Bocaccio rockfish live in the Pacific Ocean. Their backs are spiny.

The bocaccio's spines can be poisonous.

Bocaccio rockfish eat other small fish.

Water pollution has endangered this fish. Trash and dirt in the water cause pollution.

The cape seahorse lives near South Africa. This tiny fish has one fin and a strong tail.

Seahorses move very slowly.

The cape seahorse does not have teeth or a stomach. This fish swallows its food whole.

The cape seahorse is at risk of dying out.

Australia is home to the speartooth shark. This shark is endangered.

Speartooth sharks can live in both salt water and freshwater.

This fish uses its teeth to eat smaller fish.

CARCHARIAS (PRIONODON) GLYPHIS.

The speartooth shark has more than fifty rows of teeth!

Extinct Fish

Pteraspis is extinct. It has died out. This fish had a bony shield around its head.

This creature's long, pointed snout helped it swim fast.

Pteraspis was 8 inches (20 centimeters) long. Its fossils have been found in Europe.

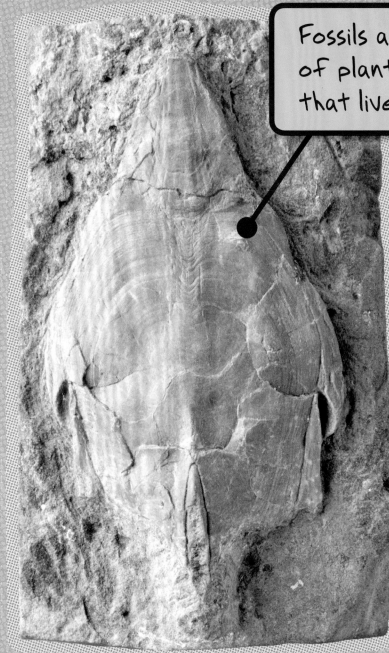

Fossils are traces of plants or animals that lived long ago.

This big fish was *Xiphactinus*.
It grew more than 13 feet
(4 m) long. That's as long
as a hippopotamus.

This fish died out
millions of years ago.

Xiphactinus had a large lower jaw. The jaw curved up. *Xiphactinus* ate large fish.

This fossil was found in Kansas.

This flat fish was called *Eobothus*. Both of its eyes were on one side of its body.

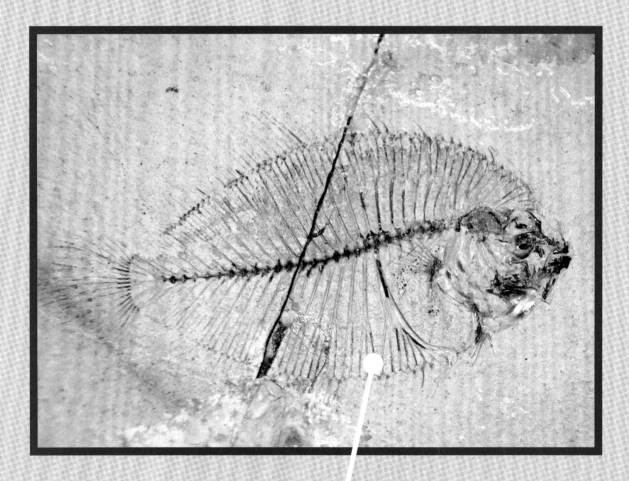

Eobothus is extinct. Its fossils have been found in Asia.

Eobothus was small. It was about 4 inches (10 cm) long.

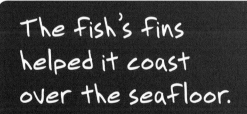

The fish's fins helped it coast over the seafloor.

This shark was longer than a school bus.

This is the largest shark ever discovered. The megalodon was more than 50 feet (16 m) long!

Megalodon lived in oceans all around the world. It ate fish and whales.

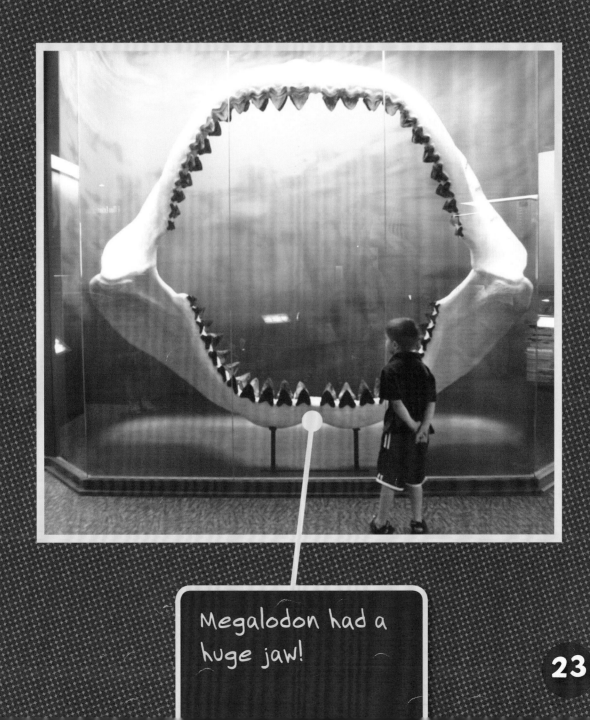

Megalodon had a huge jaw!

Enchodus was a fish with pointy teeth. It had longer front teeth called fangs. Some *Enchodus* teeth were more than 2 inches (5 cm) long.

Look at the teeth on this Enchodus fossil.

This fish could be big or small. Some *Enchodus* were only a few inches long. Others were more than 4 feet (1 m) long.

Enchodus died out millions of years ago.

Helping Endangered Fish

Many people are trying to help fish. One big way to help fish is to post signs on street drains. The signs tell people not to put trash in the drains.

This girl is marking drains.

Most street drains empty into streams or lakes. Trash in the water can make fish sick.

This sign reminds people to stop water pollution.

What You Can Do

There are many things you can do to help endangered fish.

- Don't put chemicals down the drain. The water from your drain gets dumped into lakes and oceans.
- Ask your parents to use fewer chemicals on your lawn or garden. Lawn chemicals can get into lakes and rivers too.
- Research which kinds of fish are safe to eat. Many fish that we eat are dying out. They have been fished too much. You can eat fish that are not endangered.
- Visit an aquarium to learn more about fish. Aquariums protect fish.

A Remarkable Recovery

An Okaloosa darter is less than 2 inches (5 cm) long. This tiny fish lives in Florida. It swims in streams near an air force base. Fewer than two thousand were found in 1973. Their habitat had become damaged. The fish were endangered. The air force base worked to clean the water. The fish population grew. The Okaloosa darter is no longer endangered.

Glossary

chemical: a human-made liquid. Cleaners, medicines, gasoline, oil, and paint are chemicals.

endangered: at risk of dying out

extinct: died out

fin: a thin, flat body part that a fish uses to swim

fish: a cold-blooded animal that lives underwater. Fish have backbones. Most have gills, fins, scales, and tails.

fossil: traces or hardened remains of something that lived long ago

habitat: where an animal lives

population: number of living members of a group

snout: the front of an animal's head. The nose and mouth are part of the snout.

Further Reading

Georgia Aquarium
http://animalguide
.georgiaaquarium.org

Hoare, Ben, and Tom Jackson. *Endangered Animals.* New York: DK Publishing, 2010.

Laverdunt, Damien. *Small and Tall Tales of Extinct Animals.* Wellington, NZ: Gecko Press, 2012.

National Geographic Kids: Interview with Zeb Hogan, Aquatic Ecologist
http://kids.nationalgeographic.com/kids/stories
/peopleplaces/zeb-hogan-interview

Neighborhood Explorers
http://www.fws.gov/neighborhoodexplorers

Silverman, Buffy. *Do You Know about Fish?* Minneapolis: Lerner Publications, 2010.

Index

Photo Acknowledgments

The images in this book are used with the permission of: © Secondshot/Dreamstime.com, p. 2; © Skripko Ievgen/Dreamstime.com, p. 4; © iStockphoto.com/DeepAqua, p. 5; © Lostarts/Dreamstime.com, p. 6; © Andrew J. Martinez/Science Source, p. 7; © Michael Patrick O'Neill/Science Source, pp. 8, 9; © Monterey Bay Aquarium, pp. 10, 11; © Charles Griffiths, p. 12; Brian Gratwicke/Wikimedia Commons, p. 13; Bill Harrison/Wikimedia Commons, p. 14; Harvard University, MCZ, Ernst Mayr Library/Biodiversity Heritage Library, p. 15; © De Agostini Picture Library/Getty Images, pp. 16, 18; © Colin Keates/Dorling Kindersley/Getty Images, pp. 17, 24; © Bruce R. Bennett/The Palm Beach Post/ZUMAPRESS/Alamy, p. 19; © paleo_bear/flickr.com, p. 20; © Mark Doherty/Dreamstime.com, p. 21; © Christian Darkin/Science Source, p. 22; TOM UHLENBROCK/KRT/Newscom, p. 23; © Walter Myers/Stocktrek Images/CORBIS, p. 25; © Aurora Photos/Alamy, p. 26; AP Photo/Toby Talbot, p. 27; U.S. Air Force photo, p. 29; © Dr. Richard Pillans, p. 30.

Front Cover: © Catmando/Shutterstock.com (top); © Norbert Probst/imagebroker.net/SuperStock (bottom)

Main body text set in Johann Light 30/36.